THIS JOURNAL BELONGS TO

INTRODUCTION

In meditation, I asked my higher guides what they wanted to express in this introduction. The first words that popped to mind were, "Tell them their light matters." Then came an image of street lamps. Here is the story that guidance asked me to share with you …

In cities, where many people congregate, there are many lamps close together. Well-lit streets are fairly easy to navigate. Along roads that are less travelled, the street lights are farther apart. Travellers brave enough to steer away from where the masses gather, to venture along a rarer path, rely more upon the light that each lamp brings. If a lamp on an outlying road goes out, its absence is far more noticeable. In the sunshine or by the light of a lamp, the beauty of the path that weaves through the sacred wilds of nature would be appreciated. That same path is so much harder to navigate in darkness and may even seem frightening.

This metaphor reminds us of the spiritual purpose in each of our unique paths. Although the mainstream may not be with us yet, there are many travellers who need our light as they shift from fearfully clinging to majority thinking into the courageous individuality that will allow their souls to guide them along a path unknown to the mind, but intuitively recognised by the heart. Our light matters for our own journey, but in all true spiritual journeys, there is a greater purpose — and that is to help all beings.

When we are doing our inner work and the going gets tough, remembering our spiritual responsibility is a good idea. Knowing others are depending on us can help us find the strength and courage we didn't realise we had. There is also the beautiful truth that to those of whom much is asked, much is given. The expression usually goes the other way around — to those whom much is given, much is required! I take comfort in remembering it goes both ways.

When we sense a healing task that seems great, we can be certain the Universe will provide all the resources as we need them. To the mind concerned about falling into selfishness, it is soothing to know that in our own liberation, spiritual success and inner peace, we can help others more. We have more to share and don't have to go chasing after anything, as the Universe knows what we need and delivers it with loving wisdom and benevolent grace.

This leads us to the essence of the *Crystal Mandala Oracle*, which is about channelling the divine power of heaven and earth. There is an extraordinary spiritual blessing latent in every human being. It has the potential to become something of a divine live wire, channel or vital circuit that is plugged into the celestial realms and the physical body of the earth. This blessing allows energies to flow along our spinal columns and through our nervous systems, chakras and souls, transmitting divine frequencies in accord with our choices. If we choose to take a spiritual path and learn how to integrate our dark and light sides, to accept our humanity with compassion and to amplify the positive gifts of our souls, we are stepping up to fulfil the spiritual potential we have as human beings.

In numerous spiritual traditions, including the Vedic teachings of India, Tibetan Buddhism and Western mystery schools, it is said the gods fight to be granted a human body as a human incarnation has the greatest potential for spiritual progression. What can be attained in a lifetime is, perhaps, unsurpassable. One only has to look at the accomplishments of some of the truly loving and great souls on earth to realise this idea holds truth.

Like an advanced masters' program (pun intended!) rather than a childminding service, earth school can be tough. There are many things that seem real here, that are only real if we make them so. The wilder and vaster our minds and emotional fields, the stormier the inner seas that we are learning to tame and use wisely. Learning to honour our emotions without becoming completely overtaken by them is hard. Learning not to overthink or allow our minds to dominate our hearts and steal our inner peace is even harder.

These are not complicated concepts, and yet in their simplicity they can literally take lifetimes upon lifetimes to master. We are not to be discouraged though. Often, when someone I am working with is making a breakthrough of some kind, Spirit is in a joyful uproar of celebration — just as Spirit is every time we choose wisely, act with love, are kind to ourselves and others, and choose peace and trust over fear and doubt. When we do fall into ego and stuff things up, Spirit responds with compassion, encouragement and respect. Remember, with humour and kindness, that mistakes will occur in the process of learning the lessons we were spiritually ambitious and divinely badass enough to incarnate into earth school for!

Throughout this journal you will find six healing processes. These can be done at any time you are drawn to do so. They can be done relatively quickly, or you can go deep and take longer if you choose. It is best to set aside some time for yourself, turn off mobile phones and other devices, keep the lighting soft and wear comfortable clothing. For optimal results, aim for a space where you can go into your journey and not be distracted by the external world.

My profound gratitude for the messages of love and support that higher guidance has provided for me over the years is a big motivation for me to create and share its wisdom. I do this in many ways so that people can be drawn to what they are drawn to, and drink at the loving well of soul nourishment that higher guidance provides for all beings willing to sate their spiritual thirst. Time and time again, they astonish, delight and humble me with their humour, insight, kindness, generosity and absolute devotion to every single being I work with. I know that this love, respect and protection is offered to all who want to receive it.

In working with this journal, you will be giving your soul a chance to breathe, express and create with the loving support of the incredible divine energies of crystals, angels, the ascended masters and the goddesses. I hope you come to trust in the importance of your journey and to know just how supported you are by the Universe. There is so much beauty and light within you and that is only going to increase as you walk your path, even when it seems diving into the darkness is the way to make spiritual progress.

We do need to remind each other that we have all the protection, encouragement and resources we need to fulfil our divine potential; and that the Universe is taking utter delight in the path each one of us has chosen. May you remember that. Find peace and allow your soul to continue to shine the light that guides humanity from fear to love.

Namaste,

Alana

The earth loves you without condition. She nurtures every aspect of life into existence, including you — from the life that dwells within your body to the path that will best fulfil your soul destiny.

There are many ways to be empowered. Spiritual power enables you to trust in your higher guidance no matter what appears to be happening in your life. Psychological power enables you to evolve your beliefs. Emotional power processes feelings into wisdom. Physical power strengthens you to act on matters that serve your life path.

Power can be misused when it serves one's immediate needs rather than love. When one chooses to serve love in all things, something marvellous happens — as the needs of others are met, personal needs are met, also.

You will know when you are using your power to serve love because it will strengthen your heart. You will be able to step forward on your life path and express yourself in a clearer, stronger, more-empowered way. As your light shines brighter, you will be helping others more, too.

Every human personality has its strengths and its less-helpful qualities. The less-favourable aspects of your character are not bad. They are gifts from the Universe you are encouraged to pay attention to so you can lovingly grow.

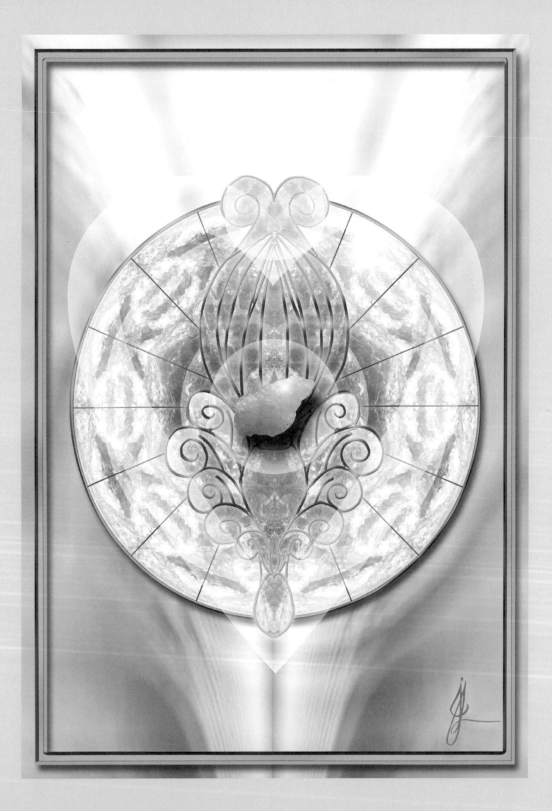

Modern culture often finds it difficult to trust in the wisdom of nature. In nature, cycles of activity are followed by cycles of rest — and this is repeated over and over with wondrous results. This lack of trust can lead to a suspicion of restfulness and judge it as weakness rather than wisdom. To manifest big, beautiful, divine dreams in this world, and to continue to do so for the rest of your long, loving life, you will need to claim your right to rest.

Experimenting with whatever brings you rest and replenishment is part of your path of self-love and personal development. Rather than getting frustrated or angry with yourself when you need rest, claim the strength to be kind and respectful to yourself. Learn how to meet your needs.

A prayer for rest: I call upon the Crystal Angel of Aragonite and Archangel Remiel. Thank you for the divine healing gift of rest. I choose to see, know and feel that rest is a way to serve love, to honour the gift of my body and mind, to express love for myself and to respect the loving, creative intelligence of the divine feminine that moves in cycles of creation and rest. So be it.

A cleansing vow: I choose of my own free will, through this and
any lifetime, and through all layers of my being, to release any fear,
resistance, guilt or shame about my need to rest.

*Acceptance is the key to transformation — even when a situation
seems challenging. It is wise to accept what is happening and then
ask how you can best respond. Acceptance doesn't mean giving up
the fight. It means learning to fight the true issue from the heart, and
growing with trust in life's guiding hand.*

A vow of trust: I choose of my own free will, through this and any lifetime, and through all layers of my being, to release programs, memories, learned behaviours and thought patterns based in distrust. I clear these at the deepest levels of my being. I now choose to embrace life through unconditional acceptance. I know life loves me and serves me to fulfil my divine destiny with mercy and compassion.

An affirmation for acceptance: Acceptance brings peace to my heart
as I embrace my unique and perfect gift of life.

Everything that is happening is part of the divine plan.
Trust that the Universe knows what it is doing and is always working
for your greatest good and the greatest good of all beings.

The key to claiming your divine life purpose is to know who you are. Knowing, loving and accepting that self, will allow your natural development and expression in the world to take place. As you accept your individuality, you will understand how natural it is for you to fulfil your life purpose and divine destiny.

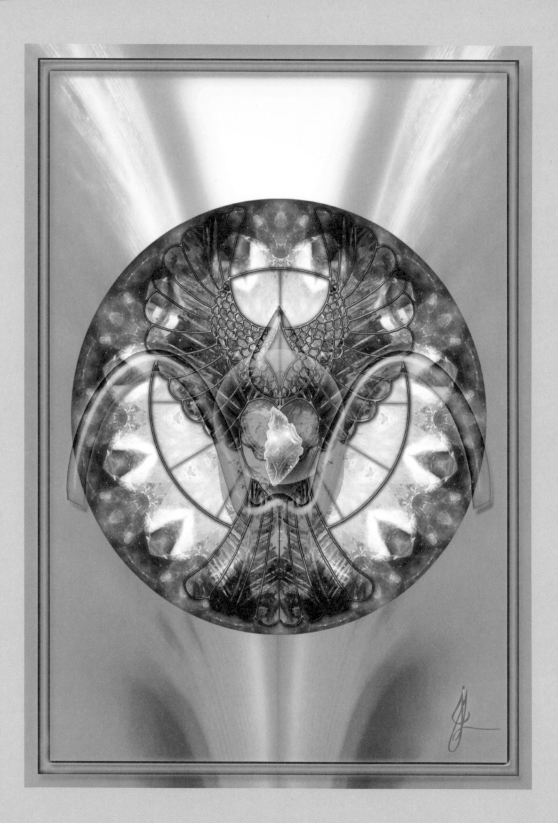

ARCHANGEL METATRON
AND THE CRYSTAL ANGEL OF CLEAR QUARTZ

For reconnecting with your inner power to fulfil your soul path

Do you feel disempowered in areas of your life? Are there steps you would like to take, and part of you is willing but other parts are in doubt? By working with the loving Crystal Angel of Clear Quartz and the powerful Archangel Metatron, you can connect with the ever-present stream of divine power that lies within you. The bigger your spiritual tasks, the more helpful dipping into this refreshing, inspiring inner-river of sacred light and healing energy will be. Whenever the Universe asks something of you spiritually, you are given the tools, resources, abilities, talents, guidance, assistance and protection to fulfil that mission — and so much more. An important step toward empowering yourself to fulfil your destiny—and this includes dealing with the twists and turns on your life path—is asking for and allowing yourself to receive, divine help.

To integrate this guidance, you may like to say this invocation now: *"I call upon the Crystal Angel of Clear Quartz and Archangel Metatron who love me unconditionally. Thank you for divine healing around all aspects of my expression of power. I now choose to see, know and feel that I am a powerful being that serves love. It is natural for me to realise my inner power and to feel safe expressing it to serve love in all ways. Through my own free will, so be it."*

To further integrate this guidance, write a list of any situations or beliefs you feel are obstacles or lessons for you around the issue of power. Once you have written your list, say the following out loud: *"I choose of my own free will, through this and any lifetime, and through all layers of my being, to release any fear, doubt, guilt or shame over the use or abuse of power by myself or others. I now dedicate myself to receiving the gift of divine power, and to using it wisely and in service to my life path, for the greater good. Through divine mercy and unconditional love, so be it."*

Scrunch up your piece of paper. If you wish, you can rip it up and throw it in the recycling bin. This is a way of casting off the items on your list. If you have written in your journal and don't want to tear out the page, simply put a big cross through it or scribble all over it (let your inner child do that) with the intention of cancelling it out.

Bow your head and say: *"May divine love heal all expressions of power, within all layers of my being, within all sentient beings. May all power serve love, so that every being can be happy and free. According to divine wisdom, so be it."*

Finish your healing process with this affirmation, said aloud three times: *"I express my power on the path of love and grow my divine presence in the world."*

There are as many ways to live your life in service to love, light and power as there are stars in the sky. Even more! Making decisions that reflect your values matters more than having another understand your lifestyle and choices.

The only people with any power to judge, control or hold you back from your destiny are those you empower to do so. At any moment you can liberate yourself from a fearful influence by choosing to love yourself no matter what and committing unconditionally to that which has meaning for you.

When you love yourself enough to be open and forthright about who you are, without needing to convince anyone of anything, but just being willing to be yourself and to share that with the world, your pathway to divine success materialises.

Your path and your purpose are as individual as you are.

A prayer for the freedom to be yourself: I choose of my own free will, through this and any lifetime, and through all layers of my being, to release any fear, shame, judgement, guilt, ridicule and suffering I have ever experienced about being an individual, about being different, about expressing who I truly am. I choose to forgive and free myself unconditionally from all such experiences, now.

An affirmation of your uniqueness and worth: I am a unique, authentic, radiant being, living true to my values with commitment and divine support. I honour who I am, and the Universe honours me.

There are times when not knowing is helpful. Not knowing the bigger picture can help you stay focused on what you need to do right now. A preoccupation with the future can distract you from the work that needs to be accomplished in the present. It can unwittingly slow your progress and delay the very future you want to draw closer.

So much can change in a short time. Knowing all that is ahead of you might throw you into fear, but when you come to that same future, in its own time, with acceptance, equanimity and trust, the same events may empower and inspire you. The Universe knows what you need and when you will best benefit from seeing what is happening from a higher perspective.

An affirmation for timely revelations: May divine love bring truth to all beings at the perfect time and in the perfect way, so every being can manifest their divine potential and be happy and free. According to divine compassion, so be it.

*It takes courage to connect with your inner world, to go deep
into the truth of your pain and to bring love to those wounds so
a healing current can transform and free you from the past. It
takes maturity to live with depth, to look beyond the surface and
to refuse to give up on your journey. When something difficult is
asked of you, it is time to grow.*

The sun is setting on what has been. A sweet promise of new life and renewed happiness is in the air.

An invocation for releasing your notion of going it alone: I now accept the truth that I have unconditionally loving support from the Universe, so all my needs may be met. I am assisted in fulfilling my divine destiny in every way possible.

You have many loving words to share and a higher consciousness to be.
In your own way, in your own world, in your own relationships,
you are a light bearer and a bringer of truth.

Others might not understand and may resist or even attack in fear, but in truth, you cannot be harmed. You shall always be what you are, and no-one can ever take that away from you. No matter how many times you have been blocked, denied, dismissed or abused, you find your way back to the truth of your heart. Again, and again, you have learned that your spirit is indestructible.

You shall not be cast down. The love in you is stronger than the fear, rejection, doubt or resistance in any other. You have no need to convince anyone of anything. You have your own words to speak and a truth to be. It is safe to be seen for who and what you are.

If you are within transformation—perhaps one that is deeply challenging—and you cannot see an end in sight or are worried that the changes are going to be devastating, have faith. Yes, this storm is wild, but it is filled with grace. You are being helped. You shall come through this. The storm was needed because a gentler method would not have been sufficient to free you.

ANGEL CALIEL

AND THE CRYSTAL ANGEL OF POLYCHROME JASPER

For when the path has become intense and serious and you need some joyful relief

Doing inner work can be very intense. If we didn't have discipline and take it seriously, we would lack the follow through required to deal with difficult matters of the heart as well as the courage and strength required to confront situations that need to change. This is important and deserves respect. However, we also need lightness, a sense of humour and opportunities to play, so that our inner child is not unwittingly shut down. If this happens, the wellspring of your joy, creativity, curiosity and energy to laugh, flirt, play or take chances will seem to have dried up. When it is time to consciously reconnect with the childlike quality of play, you will be guided to lighten the demands on yourself, at least for a time, and to remember that you are not alone. There are loving beings in this Universe that are with you every step of the way. When you take time to stop and smell the flowers, you will have more energy for other matters, too. Laughter—always with kindness—doesn't take us away from the serious nature of our healing journey. It helps us soften the darkness and open the way for swifter healing to take place.

To integrate this guidance, you may like to say this invocation now: *"I call upon the Crystal Angel of Polychrome Jasper and Angel Caliel. Thank you for the divine healing gift of sacred play. I honour my disciplined nature and the strength of my commitment. I honour the need to balance this with freedom, spontaneity and joy. In receiving your gift of sacred play, I open my heart to the light and share that light through my laughter. Through my own free will, so be it."*

To further integrate this guidance, do something that your inner child will think is fabulous — and perhaps your most serious adult self would raise an eyebrow at. It may be making music with pots and pans, playing with a pet in the garden, dancing wildly in your lounge room or singing kitchen karaoke at the top of your lungs. You can be respectful to the needs of those around you and yet still let loose. Choose whatever feels right for your inner child in this moment. He or she may just want to lie on the floor and colour in for a while!

When you have had some fun time, say aloud: *"I choose of my own free will, through this and any lifetime, and through all layers of my being, to release any shame or guilt about laughter, play and lightness of spirit. I accept the lighthearted side of my nature because I know I am filled with depth and compassion and am capable of endurance and delight. I accept sacred play as a healing part of my life that restores me daily through delight. Through divine grace, humour and unconditional love, so be it."*

You can finish your healing process with this affirmation, said aloud three times, and perhaps with a wiggle of the hips at the conclusion: *"Every day has time for sacred play! Hip, hip, hooray!"*

*To shed conditioning, one layer at a time, takes courage, as you must
trust in a self you do not yet fully recognise.*

If you feel an inner call for growth, trust it. Your wild tiger spirit is rising and lifting you out of the world you have known, into an increasingly vibrant, radiant and loving life. Roar loud and proud. Your kindred, tiger-spirited souls will hear you and be drawn to your light.

You can become so accustomed to carrying something that it feels natural to do so. It isn't until you no longer have that burden that you realise how much easier your life is without it. Attachment is a powerful force. However, love is far more powerful and helps us let go.

If you are asked to hand over the scraps you believe to be treasures,
it is only so you can be gifted with a sacred feast.

If you have made leaps in the past, only to land flat on your face rather than gracefully on your feet, leave that behind you now. Everything you have experienced in your life has led you towards this moment in time. You are not the same person you were before. You are stronger, wiser and readier for the beautiful adventure life has in store for you.

You may feel afraid or uncertain if you listen to your mind. Give some love to your mind. It might need your comfort and reassurance. Then listen to your heart.

An affirmation for the courage to take a leap of faith:
The Universe responds to my every action with an outpouring
of love, assistance, encouragement and opportunity, which I
gratefully receive. It is safe for me to take a leap of faith.

When you place your hand on your heart to honestly and simply ask the Universe for healing on whatever issue troubles you, you are using the power of your heart to trigger an outpouring of creative resources from the Universe to you.

If you compare yourself to others and feel your voice is not as powerful, loving, wise or somehow not enough, stop immediately. Your truths are your own. You have been created according to a divine design. You—and your voice—are as you are meant to be.

Our struggles in life can be challenging enough without adding unnecessary guilt, shame or judgement into the mix. There can be a temptation to wonder why you are not getting something, what you are doing wrong or to blame karma. Yet when there is struggle, there is also opportunity for spiritual growth that can show you how to let go and live in a gentler way. Accept your struggles with dignity whilst opening your heart to a kinder way.

*Intellectually, you may know that the Universe loves you and is
helping you always, but emotionally, you may feel insecure, uncertain
or challenged. Practice allowing yourself to choose relaxation and
trust, and you will find it much easier to recognise (and enjoy) how
incredibly creative and intelligent life is — and how amazing your
spiritual journey is, too!*

Constraint can be a way for your soul to build spiritual muscle, i.e.
trust, endurance and the sacrifice of instant gratification for long-
term success. It is not essential, but it is a way to love life a little more,
engage with what is and resist a little less.

Do everything you can, and then let go, again and again. Trust that higher will is working for your best interests and will help you manifest your most soul-satisfying success at the perfect time and in the perfect way.

Discernment is not judgement. Discernment means having a neutral, non-judging and detached perspective. Discernment helps you recognise the true value, potential, intention and capacity of the people and situations in your life. It is a way to allow reality to become clear to you. You can then choose whether to invite an energy in or to let it move on.

Sacred alchemy always starts with the alchemist. Will and belief empower the alchemist to continue their sacred work, even when it is misunderstood or dismissed by those that don't know better.

Whatever you want to change in your physical world can change.
It requires a commitment to consciousness and growth as well as
unconditional trust in the process. Don't give up until all is as you wish it
to be. You must believe in yourself and in the power of the Divine.

ASCENDED MASTER LADY NADA

AND THE CRYSTAL ANGEL OF RHODOCHROSITE

For when you feel it's difficult to be sensitive in this world of ours

In our upside-down culture, people who are sensitive are often told to toughen up as though it is a weakness, but sensitivity is a strength, a skill and a gift. Being able to feel and tune in to subtle energies requires us to develop our sensitivity. Despite the fear that heightened sensitivity makes it harder to live in this world, its continued development increases our ability to be nourished and nurtured by subtle healing frequencies, and to be positively affected on all levels of body, mind and soul in ways that those not as open cannot so easily experience. It is said that the sweetest fruit is at the top of the tree, suggesting that a bit of extra effort will bring a greater reward. This can certainly be the case for those willing to work through the challenges of being sensitive before they realise the extraordinary benefits.

Sometimes, when we take the path of the sensitive, we need comfort along the way. I remember when I was a very young woman with my first boyfriend and staying at his family's place for the first time. His relationship with his violent father was difficult for him to manage. The environment in the house and in our hearts, was filled with tension, pain and anxiety. One afternoon it felt almost unbearable, so we lay down side by side, hand in hand, and did a meditation to call in Lady Nada. This soothed away the pain and allowed us to reconnect with a sense of love, peace and healing. Ever since that time, I have had a deep trust in Lady Nada's ability to comfort all who call upon her.

To integrate this guidance, you may like to say this invocation now: *"I call upon the Crystal Angel of Rhodochrosite and Ascended Master Lady Nada who love me unconditionally. Thank you for the divine blessing of sensitivity. May I trust what I perceive with serenity in my heart and mind. May I choose to respond with compassion and yet maintain firm boundaries. May I always remember that though I may perceive so much, I have the power to choose that which will enter my field of energy, and that which will—through the power of my own free will—leave and not return. I open to your comforting presence now, through unconditional love and divine mercy."*

If you can, take a few moments to rest with your hands on your heart. You can listen to music or just settle and rest. Then say aloud: *"I choose of my own free will, through this and any lifetime, and through all layers of my being, to release any fear, judgement or shame around my sensitivity. I trust my perceptions. I trust in my wise, serene and firm responses to all I perceive. I invite unconditional love to enter my life for my greatest good. I now command anything that is not of unconditional love to leave my field and never return. I forgive and release you in goodwill. Go in peace. Through divine grace and unconditional love, may all beings be happy and free. So be it."*

You may like to contemplate the gifts that sensitivity brings you. One way to do this is to imagine a garden. Although your sensitivity may make you more nervous about unintentionally stepping on a fairy or disrupting a spider's web, it also gives you the ability to hear celestial music in the sounds of nature and to be healed by the breath of Gaia as it weaves through the trees. It can be easier to relax in gratitude when giving yourself a chance to connect with nature.

You can finish your healing process with this affirmation, said aloud three times: *"I am sensitive to the loving spiritual presence that communicates messages of peace and empowerment to me daily. My sensitivity is a way to know the deeper beauty of life — and I love it. I am protected, and it is safe for me to feel."*

A message from the Masters: "You have endured lessons of patience. You have learned that spiritual progress can be made even when results are not immediately obvious. You have learned to trust and have a willingness to surrender your personal desires into a larger plan. We know what you are capable of, and we now invite you to step into the next level of empowered service to the greater plan that is unfolding in divine love."

Trust in your abilities. You do not have to compare or compete with any other. The people, places and situations you are here to help this lifetime have been selected at a higher level, long before you incarnated. Your light will attract those you are destined to assist.

There is an exquisite intelligence to divine design, a way for every aspect of every being to serve the great plan of love. There is not one part of you that is unacceptable to the Divine. Heal, grow, and do so from a place of love, not rejection.

If you have felt ostracised, abandoned, rejected or criticised by a system in which you have tried to serve, take heart. The Universe is guiding you towards your rightful place, your home upon the earth, your soul tribe. All your experiences are helpful to the soul, so there is no need to force yourself to fit in to a way that is not resonant with your heart. Have faith. All things come in time.

If you have received a message—either directly or through someone who believes it has come from the spiritual worlds—and what you see, feel or hear makes you feel bad or is based in fear, then it is not from the higher spiritual worlds. Genuine divine guidance is loving. Anything that makes you feel disconnected from love or causes you to feel bad about yourself, is not higher guidance.

A prayer for releasing any pain surrounding your spirituality:
Through this and any lifetime, and through all layers of my
being, I choose to release any experience, memory or belief
connected to spiritual abuse, manipulation or persecution, as
well as feelings of disconnection from or abandonment by the
Divine. I now open myself completely to divine grace.

A prayer for global comfort: May divine love awaken the fullness of
spiritual connection in the hearts of all living beings.

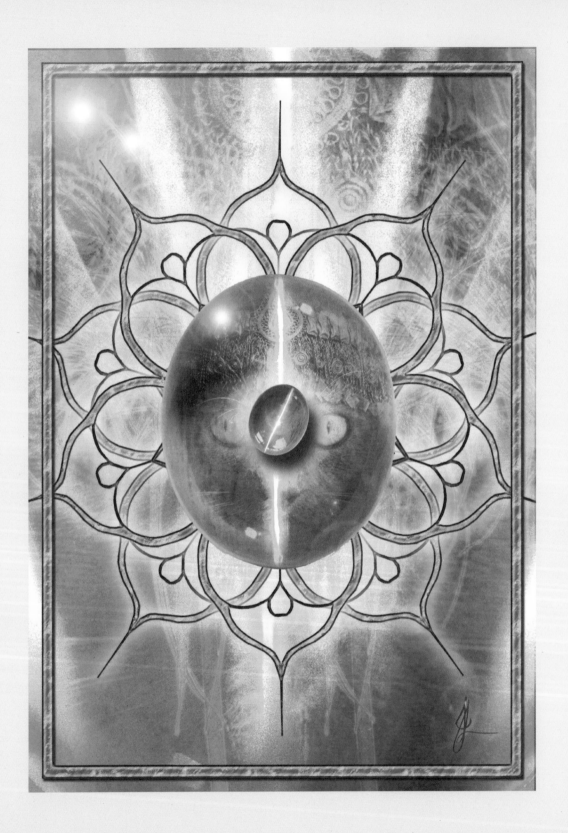

Any kind of grounding is an act of will, especially for those that find it easier to fly free and soar amongst stars, ideas, other realms or subtle energies. We must want to be grounded. Being in love with the earth and knowing that foundation, allows us to manifest our visions and can help us summon the will to be in the here and now.

Sacred rebels are free spirits who don't need to control others or be controlled to feel safe. They know life is crazy, mysterious, beautiful and uncontrollable, and that we can either hide in fear from the wild and magnificent, or show up, jump on and go for a ride we'll never forget.

You will know when you have met the right people. You will recognise them as your soul brothers and sisters. You can support each other in your refusal to fall in line with the mainstream groupthink that holds too many in fear, uncertainty and ignorance of their divine nature. Together, you will stir things up, create a loving fuss and refuse to be told you cannot do what makes your soul come to life.

An affirmation to help you march to your own beat: I honour the divine rebel within. I give myself permission to live my truths with wisdom, compassion and boldness.

For the weary and anxious mind, unconditional trust can bring great relief. The idea that you don't have to keep worrying as everything is going to work out with divine grace according to a higher plan can soothe away mental anguish and emotional suffering.

A global prayer to heal mother issues: I choose of my own free will, through this and any lifetime, and through all layers of my being, to thoroughly release, forgive and free myself from any wound, experience or belief to do with mothering and trust. May broken trust be healed. May distrust give way to peace. May all beings feel the healing relief of unconditional trust in the love that the Universe has for them.

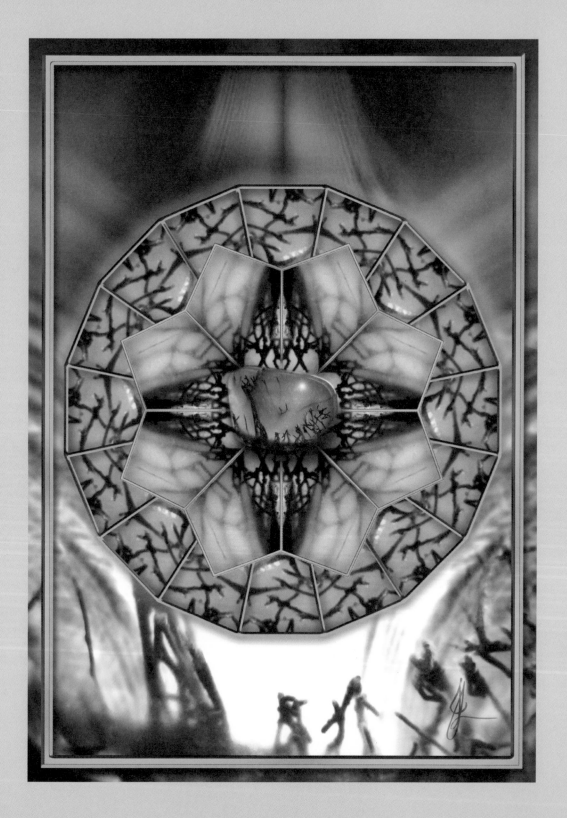

ASCENDED MASTER KUTHUMI

AND THE CRYSTAL ANGEL OF MOSS AGATE

*For when you feel like a spiritual orphan in search of a more genuine
and loving soul tribe*

Acknowledging when I have outgrown a relationship or a group and keeping
faith at those times has been one of the challenges of my journey — even when
remaining connected would prevent me from honestly and authentically being
myself. In such situations, I have had to take a leap of faith and let go. Later in life,
I would sometimes meet up with those people again and we would be able to relate
in a much more honest way. At other times, I never see them again. In letting go, I
would sometimes move swiftly into a more loving connection with others. At other
times, I was alone for a time and left wondering if I had made a mistake.

Over several decades, I have learned that when we listen to the voice of the soul,
there are no mistakes. Things may not go as we expect, but there is usually a simple
issue at play — divine timing. Some of the most profound, loving, life-affirming
and healing relationships have come into my life many years after I began wishing
for them. Sometimes many, many years later! It has always been a case of the
person in question not quite being ready for me when I realised my need for them.
Circumstances had to unfold before we could even meet. So, during those years of
wondering whether the Universe had heard my prayers, it was already answering
them. I just needed to have faith and learn how to love and care for myself in the
meantime, which was quite a helpful lesson anyway.

If you have been feeling out of sync with those around you, you may just need some time out to recalibrate, so you can bring your energies back into the mix and continue to be a positive influence in your communities. However, there are times when you may need to cut loose and move on. There's no need to fear either of these things. Your heart will guide you through the loving wisdom of the Universe that resides within it.

To integrate this guidance, you may like to say this invocation now: *"I call upon the Crystal Angel of Moss Agate and Ascended Master Kuthumi who love me unconditionally. May all be lovingly guided with divine mercy and unconditional love into the sacred ecosystem that will allow them to fulfil their divine potential. May all beings find their true home in life, where they can love and be loved, naturally attract those meant to be in their life and fulfil their divine potential for the greatest good. Through unconditional love and my own free will, so be it."*

If you wish to further integrate this guidance, you can write or say a beautiful prayer to those that may be bringing up painful issues for you at this time. Simply write or say their name, followed by this prayer: *"May there be peace and forgiveness between us. I love you and I want the best for you and for myself."*

When you are ready to complete the final step, say the following aloud: *"I choose of my own free will, through this and any lifetime, and through all layers of my being, to release all fears of abandonment, social isolation, rejection, betrayal and of feeling I do not belong to a sacred home and unconditionally loving family. I release all such wounds, memories and associated beliefs, now. I choose of my own free will to embrace the reality of the sacred ecosystem where I have a place, a purpose and a presence that contributes to the greater good. I trust the Universe to guide me into the sacred ecosystem within which I can best fulfil my divine potential and serve love, now. Through divine grace and unconditional love, so be it."*

If you sense great pain and suffering around you, do not become afraid. You are fulfilling the spiritual task of helping those who are lost. You are the lighthouse shining in the darkness.

If you allow the negativity of those in fear to become part of how you view yourself, you will undermine yourself. In doing so, you allow negativity to sabotage your spiritual light. This can happen when you take to heart the critical remark of someone more interested in criticising others than focusing on their own personal healing. Have compassion for others, but remember, your compassion is not complete unless it extends to yourself, too.

The fierce face of the Divine Mother is trained upon your precious heart. She will intervene on your behalf. Do not doubt the extent and power of her love for you. Nothing can overcome it. She always wins.

An affirmation for the lion goddess within your heart: I am a bold,
lion-hearted lover of life, fierce with passionate purpose.

If you want to change your experience of life, change your frequency. You will start repelling or feeling repelled by people, behaviours or places that once may have enthralled and enslaved your body and mind. Fear will not be able to grip you in the same way as it could at lower frequencies. You will have more energy to deal with life and attract more experiences that increase the good feelings you have about yourself and your love for the world.

The easiest way to change your frequency is to consciously choose your words. If you find yourself dwelling on a negative, switch it up. Look at the same situation as a way you can learn. You can be curious, open and willing to grow so the situation can evolve into something far more enjoyable. Instead of feeling victimised or defeated, adopt a positive attitude and be determined to empower yourself with your attitude.

Speak your truths and your desires. Speak of what you wish to experience.
When you catch yourself thinking or speaking in a voice other than love, be
kind and change it. Your words have power. Use them wisely.

GODDESS TARA

AND THE CRYSTAL ANGEL OF TIBETAN QUARTZ

For when you need to deflect negativity so you can continue to shine

Sometimes, jealousy of your light may come from those in separation who have forgotten it is the divinity in them that recognises the divinity in you! Perhaps they have become so stuck in the illusions of the world that they believe they will miss out when others seem to be in abundant flow. From an erroneous view of scarcity, they may believe the only way they can feel better about themselves, is to exert power over and destroy someone or something that is bringing up their insecurities.
In such instances, it is important to sustain your focus on the divine light within you. You may be aware of the pain or negativity that is directed towards you, but you need not dwell on it. Tara, the mother of divine light from the Tibetan Buddhist tradition, is a powerful protector and saviour goddess of endless compassion. In situations where there is much pain, there needs to be an increase of compassion to soak it up. Tara can do this when someone cannot process their pain and attempts to blame you for it instead.

Rather than being dragged into the suffering of another, you can focus with delight on Tara, and allow her tremendously powerful field of wisdom to lift you and offer healing to all involved. Any action that allows you to bring more of Tara's presence into the world is going to earn some serious spiritual brownie points for you and benefit all beings. In a way, you can thank the person who might have led you to this practice today as you take refuge in the generosity and power of the Divine Mother.

To integrate this guidance, say this invocation: *"I call upon the Crystal Angel of Tibetan Quartz and Goddess Tara who love me unconditionally. Thank you for the divine, healing empowerment of your presence. Please surround me with your unconditional divine protection and field of fierce, compassionate grace. I thank you for protecting the expression of my light in the world, in my body, in my mind and in my speech. Through your divine mercy and my own free will, so be it."*

If you wish to further integrate this guidance, visualise yourself being surrounded in a beautiful green light of the Divine Mother. Imagine the light coming from her heart, filling you and creating a shield around you.

Then say aloud: *"I choose of my own free will, through this and any lifetime, and through all layers of my being, to forgive, release and deflect all fearful reactions to light. I invoke the complete protection of the Universal Mother so that my light may shine true and feed many. Through divine empowerment and unconditional love, so be it."*

Say this mantra to Tara as many times as feels good for you, *"Om Tare Tuttare Ture Swaha"* (sounds like: OM TARAY TWO TARAY TWO RAY SWAH HAH). Then, complete this healing process by relaxing in meditation for as long as you wish.

Rebirth promises a new life and a new you that is increasingly authentic, vibrant and free. It is possible for you to have this. However, rebirth requires a shamanic death. This is not physical death, but a spiritual transformation. Whatever is keeping you from living a happier, freer, more beautiful, joyous and soul-satisfying life is to be sacrificed—allowed to die—so you can be born anew.

Embrace courage and daring, because shamanic death and rebirth can frighten the mind. You will be celebrating after the process but going through it will stimulate your fears. This is supposed to happen. How will you lay your fears aside without confronting them and choosing to let them go? Do not fear your fear. Let it rise and fall away.

Let all your choices come from your heart. If it feels right for your
heart and there is joy there (even if you must search beneath the fear
of what might go wrong to find it), then do it.

Pleasure and pain are part of life. You can enjoy pleasure without fear of becoming addicted to or softened by it, so that you are no longer able to bear your pain. Knowing you have access to genuine, natural pleasure can be a way to manage pain more effectively. It might seem strange, but we can become mentally addicted to pain. Pain has its rightful place in life, but pleasure does too. Give yourself permission to take pleasure in your existence.

An encourager is a person who generates goodwill. They are not afraid of missing out. They are happy to wait at the cosmic traffic lights, so to speak, and to allow those who have a green light to go first. They know their time for a green light will come in due course, just as it shall be for everyone on the divine highway of life.

Change takes courage. We must be willing to let go of what we have known, and bear uncertainty, whilst we explore new possibilities and eventually evolve into a new way of being.

Where gentler methods aren't effective and divine timing requires change to happen now, Goddess Kali may stomp in and kick you out of the nest, so you realise you can fly. She may knock the control freak dominating your mind on the head, and temporarily set up her own divine dictatorship where she simply repeats, "Love yourself and let go," until you do just that.

GODDESS LAKSHMI

AND CRYSTAL ANGEL OF DENDRITIC AGATE

For when you want things to lighten up, flow freely and be blessed with prosperity

You may already have plenty of real-life examples of how struggle moves us farthest and quickest. We tend to be more motivated by pain than by pleasure. However, we can also cultivate enough inner motivation to attend to our path, to meditate, to work on our emotional wellbeing, to show up for creative challenges, to open our hearts, to speak up, to take loving risks and so forth, without needing the Universe to push us to do it.

Even when we have grown enough to internalise our spiritual disciplines, we may still need a loving push to help us overcome the more difficult challenges. But, the more willing we are to seek and embrace spiritual growth, the more we will do so through a gentle golden grace based in abundance, flow and effortlessness. Maybe you feel ready for such a place? Maybe you are ready to work through any self-worth issues stopping you from relaxing into a life of generosity and ease?

Sometimes taking the simple path can be more confronting than doing things the hard way, especially where we are familiar with being the warrior and needing to fight every step of the way. Opening to grace will not make you soft, but it will help you realise the Universe is kind and generous. It will also make it easier for you to trust in life. This will help you move further along your path with a boldness and confidence that could not be summoned by a more hesitant heart.

There may be something specific—like a healing, resolution or creation of some kind—that you would like to open to an easier and more graceful manifestation. You may feel ready to shift your whole life into a more effortless flow. Either way, you can commune with Lakshmi, the golden goddess of the Hindu tradition, who is radiance, enlightenment, beauty, love, prosperity and grace combined.

To integrate this guidance, you may like to say this invocation now: *"I call upon the Crystal Angel of Dendritic Agate and Goddess Lakshmi. I open my heart, my mind and my soul to the generosity of your grace. I allow your gentle divine glow to flow unimpeded through me, opening me to receive and become a channel for your love to enter the world. Through unconditional love and my own free will, so be it."*

To further integrate this guidance, write a list of blessings being as generous, creative, abundant and joyful as you wish. If there are material things included on that list, make sure you include your desire to receive those items so that you can assist more people or share more happiness with the world. The more abundant, open and spiritually connected your attitude, the more the Universe can bring you what your heart desires. Have fun with your list. You may like to write some beautiful words or draw love hearts or other images around the borders of your blessings list.

Then say aloud: *"I choose of my own free will, through this and any lifetime, and through all layers of my being, to release any guilt, shame, fear or doubt about receiving. I release any fear that would have me 'hold in' rather than 'open to.' I choose to soften and gently release any experiences and related beliefs based on feeling undeserving or unworthy to receive. May all beings be blessed by the Divine to become able to receive all they need to be happy and free. May all sentient beings experience and relax into the love, generosity, abundance and grace of the Universe. So be it."*

You can finish your healing process with this mantra repeated as many times as feels good for you, *"Om Shrim Maha Lakshmiyei Swaha"* (sounds like OM SHREE MAAH-HAAH LUCK-SH-MEE-YAY SWAAH-HAAH). Complete your healing process by resting into meditation.

Integrity is developed over time. It exists when a person cares enough about the impact their words, actions and intentions have on others that they are willing to make tough calls and not always take the path that seems easiest. However, integrity doesn't make life harder. It makes it more enjoyable. Every time you exercise integrity, you will feel good about yourself.

When you act with integrity, your ability to attract what you need grows — your light and presence become more magnetic. Instead of chasing after what you think you need or want, you will stand still and draw the right people and opportunities to you.

Unplugging from mass conditioning is one of the most liberating thresholds you will go through on the spiritual path. In the same way you might imagine a cult member must deprogram their mind when they return to normal society, there is a point on the spiritual path where you realise normal society is trapped in a mindset of its own, and the freedom-loving, divine rebel in you will want out.

Do not allow fear-based reality to temper your spirit, tame your heart or dull your dreams.

If you are feeling used, abused, exploited or taken advantage of, allow your inner queen to rise and remind you of your royalty! Seek out your inner divine dignity, summon your compassion for everyone involved in the situation—including yourself—and give yourself permission to disengage from the drama.

A prayer for determination from the Goddess Isis: I choose to forgive
and free myself from any memory, experience or belief tied to
giving up. I honour the reality of my inner strength, my will to love,
and my love for life. May I be carried upon the powerful wings
of Isis who loves me unconditionally. May all beings know the
unassailable strength of love within their hearts. So be it.

Look to your life. What's happening? What's possible for you to act upon? What are you currently empowered to do? There's your divine task. Do what you can and do it now.